STAT[illegible] CONS[illegible] & GROWTH MANAGEMENT POLICY

A LEGISLATOR'S GUIDE

by
Gordon Meeks, Jr.

edited by
Sharon Schwoch

National Conference of State Legislatures
William T. Pound, Executive Director

1050 17th Street, Suite 2100
Denver, Colorado 80265

444 North Capitol Street, N.W., Suite 500
Washington, D.C. 20001

April 1990

ISBN 1-55516-455-2

Table of Contents

Acknowledgments

The Energy, Science, and Natural Resources Program of the National Conference of State Legislatures has prepared numerous reports, provided technical assistance, sponsored conferences and workshops, and responded to seemingly thousands of information requests in the past 10 years related to state land use and conservation policies. This workload has been made possible by the generous support of several foundations, particularly the David and Lucile Packard Foundation and the William and Flora Hewlett Foundation. Other sponsors have been the Andrew W. Mellon, Donner, Ford, Northwest Area, Joyce, and Jesse Smith Noyes foundations.

Work over this period of time has required the staff of the program to accumulate and continually update information on wetland, farmland, groundwater, conservation, and general natural resource management issues. This book is a culmination and summary of the author's knowledge obtained throughout these years of tracking land use issues. It is part of a project funded by the David and Lucile Packard Foundation to review state land conservation policy and provide information to legislatures developing new conservation programs and policies. The author is very grateful to the Packard Foundation for enabling this work to proceed and to the Hewlett Foundation for augmenting the basic funding level and therefore stretching the resources of the National Conference of State Legislatures for services on these issues.

Likewise, many individuals and organizations have supported the program's efforts. Space does not permit mentioning them all. But the author would be grossly remiss if he did not recognize certain individuals for consistent and enthusiastic assistance over the years. They include:

Nancy Bushwick Malloy, Resources for the Future
Deborah Schmidt, Montana Environmental Quality Council
Bob Gray, Resource Management Consultants, Inc.
John Stolzenberg, Wisconsin Legislative Council
John Helland, Minnesota House Research
Carol Baudler, The Nature Conservancy
Representative Paul Johnson, Iowa
Representative David Osterberg, Iowa
Mary Lou Munts, Wisconsin Public Service Commissioner
Sandra Batie, Virginia Tech
Russ Butcher, National Parks and Conservation Association

Jon Kusler, Association of Wetland Managers
Bill Nothdurft, resource consultant
David Peterson, Laventhol & Horwath
Frank Popper, Rutgers University
Henry Richmond, 1000 Friends of Oregon

Cheryl Runyon and John DeGrove reviewed early drafts of the document. The author owes a debt of gratitude to Larry Morandi for providing sound editorial advice and to Sharon Schwoch, who makes the author's writing easier to read and comprehend.

Preface

State land use policy has been developing rapidly. When the author first began his career in land use planning and conservation 16 years ago, there was an extensive but manageable body of literature. We have now achieved information overload. The legal and technical documentation is almost beyond imagination and is still growing. This overload of information presents a challenge to the policy specialist who must omit choice pieces of material to present a concise summary and explanation of current land use policy and management practices to an audience of policymakers with significant time constraints. This book is the author's current best effort at the objective. It will probably be superseded in short order, but it is hoped that this discussion provides an overview of current state land conservation policy and reveals at least a hint of future policy.

In addition to the information explosion, the body of state legislation has expanded dramatically. In 1980, state-mandated land use planning, much less growth management, was politically infeasible in Georgia and New Jersey. But both states, among others, have adopted programs of extensive state involvement in what was previously considered local political turf. Land conservation has been a primary motivating force, as cities have grown and consumed farmland at a dizzying pace, even during the slow growth years of the most recent recession. But increasing concern about adequate public infrastructure and services, traffic congestion, affordable housing, air quality, and other problems associated with uncoordinated urban growth has created new political consensuses and voter agitation. State legislatures are pursuing policies of land conservation and related objectives much more actively than they were a few years ago. Consequently, surveys of state land use policies and conservation programs are outdated almost before they are printed because each legislative session marks a new turning point in another state for wetlands preservation, growth management, land conservation, or parkland and critical areas management.

This book does not address federal conservation policy. Descriptions of federal authorities are available elsewhere. This guide was written as a primer on current state policies and programs on land conservation, land use, and growth management. There are four primary paths to land conservation: government regulation, public parkland acquisition, private land set asides, and cooperation between the public and private sectors using a mix of regulatory and financial management techniques. This book addresses these through summaries of state policies and case studies. In addition, it discusses social attitudes toward land, describes the history of land policy and case law, briefly explains various policy instruments, lists states that have adopted specific land conservation and regulatory policies, discusses comprehensive growth management policies, examines market and private sector conservation efforts, describes critical areas designation, and finally, illustrates how government and the private sector can cooperate to meet the seemingly opposing goals of conservation and development.

Many state actions affect land use and conservation. Local property taxes are defined by state enabling authorities and have extensive impact on the way private land is used. Capital construction (i.e., highways) of state and local government also has direct and immediate impact on land development or conservation. These actions are generally carried out with goals and objectives unrelated to land use. These issues are touched on here, but it is impractical to attempt to account for every public action that might have some effect on land because virtually every public action will have some impact on land resources. This book tries to cover those major policies and programs that were enacted specifically and intentionally to affect land use patterns or conservation.

“Property, like every other social institution, has a social function to fulfill.”

Justice B. Cardoso
The Nature of the Judicial Process

I

Introduction

In the book *Losing Ground,* Hugh Ulrich asserts that "the foundation of all economic activity [is] the production of food."[1] This would imply that land is the foundation of all wealth and, therefore, political power. These fundamental values associated with land may be directing land use policy decisions more subconsciously than overtly. It should come as no surprise then if land developments arouse keen interest and emotions. Politicians, academics, business managers, and other social leaders are often shocked and dismayed at neighborhood and community opposition to land developments that promise change. The surprise should come when there is no opposition.

Many will challenge the thesis that all wealth and power derive from land. The evidence supporting it is quite convincing, however. Food and the means of its production are the most (and over-) cited case in point. Other commodities such as building materials, minerals, and life-supporting materials (e.g., water) are land dependent.

In his book of the same name, James Hite, professor at Clemson's Strom Thurmond Institute, says that land "provides society with the essential 'room and situation' for all human activity." In our high-tech, modern society, we overlook the importance of geography to our detriment. The cost of doing business is still determined largely by spatial and geographic factors such as costs of raw materials, transportation of raw and finished commodities, access to labor and markets, and the sociocultural environment. In fact, the very political, social, and cultural conditions within which we work and conduct business are largely creations of an earlier time when our connection to the land was more pronounced. Modern telecommunications, computing, and transportation technologies may have loosened our economic dependence on land, but regional economies and infrastructure are still based on historic land values, policies, and traditional philosophies.

The way our land is used affects and is affected by broad and fundamental social and political conditions. Tax or international trade policy, in reality, may have more impact on overall land use patterns than explicit land use policies. We have written our tax codes, however, primarily to derive enough revenue to run governments, not to affect land use. Implications of how taxes influence land use patterns are obscure. We do not analyze every potential fallout of seemingly unrelated policies, and their impacts on land use are usually ignored.

The history of land use has been determined by a nomadic approach to its development. Throughout most of our history, land has been relatively abundant. Consequently, immediate convenience has outweighed matching use of the land with its suitability. We have assumed that land is readily renewable and reusable. In a practical sense, it is not. It may take decades or centuries for stone or organic matter to be turned into soil for growing food. Similarly, urban *renewal,* a synthetic process (as opposed to natural), is becoming cost prohibitive both economically and politically. And industrial development of almost any land parcel is becoming less acceptable socially. As population increases and as modern lifestyles require more land consumption per capita, the amount of land available for mutually exclusive uses becomes more limited—hence, the level of controversy over any change in land use.

Former Department of Energy Secretary James R. Schlesinger was referring to modern land use politics when he said that "we have reached the stage of participatory democracy where almost everyone in the society can say 'no,' but no one can say 'yes.'" Investment banker Felix Rohatyn said the land policy system in the United States "has become all checks and no balances.... Today we could not build our road system, the TVA, or the Manhattan project." No doubt, plenty of activists would be happy if none of these projects had ever been undertaken.

This gridlock of land use has revitalized a trend toward more state involvement in land use policy. Growth strategies commissions are conducting hearings and deliberating growth management policies in Massachusetts, Virginia, Maryland, and Washington while legislators and governors in other states are considering creation of similar commissions. Georgia passed legislation last year that requires all local governments to complete comprehensive land use plans. These initiatives in state land conservation and management are described explicitly as attempts to "balance" competing interests in land use.

Whereas growth management programs adopted by states in the 1960s and 1970s were driven largely by land conservation motives, programs in the 1980s appear to be stimulated additionally by fiscal and economic development considerations. A meeting of the minds is occurring among environmental conservationists and economic developers in the states where growth management has been adopted. Environmentalists have recognized that land use policies must accommodate economic development if conservation goals are to be achieved. Correspondingly, developers are acknowledging that quality-of-life factors are critical to sustaining healthy growth. These moves toward moderation by traditional opponents are being explicitly encouraged by the makeup and agendas of growth strategies commissions, which incorporate the mediation process in their structure.

Mediation may be a useful method to resolve specific conflicts over land allocation, but conflict is an inherent aspect of land resource allocation. Human history is essentially one of territorial wars, social revolutions for control of the factors of production (including land), and political oscillation between opposing ideological philosophies. Some scholars have researched and characterized the nature of land use conflicts.

Sidney Plotkin, author of *Keep Out: The Struggle for Land Use Control,* characterizes modern land use conflicts as functions of an inherently contradictory capitalist economic system. In his words, land use conflict results from the dual motives of capitalism: "expansion versus exclusion." Capitalist expansion is associated with economic (land) development, and exclusion is equated with private property rights, both of which are basic philosophical foundations of capitalism. They collide, according to Plotkin, when the economic need to consume land conflicts with the private rights to keep the unwanted out.

In Plotkin's words, our economic system is

> constantly pushed and pulled in opposite directions. The twists of expansion are inextricably connected with and opposed by turns of exclusion. Nothing is more important to legitimacy than growth, yet nothing would be more illegitimate than a wholesale attack on the exclusionary rights of property and community self-protection. Exclusion is the most rational social condition of class-driven expansion, but nothing would be more irrational from a corporate standpoint than to permit small landowners and communities to dictate the paths of development.[2]

The upshot of this paradox is that "when these forces collide, people come to be against what they have been for, and for what they have been against." Threatened with the loss of their sense of community and pastoral land values, social liberals may favor policies that preserve environmental values (open space and scenic vistas) but that also have the side effect of discriminating against racial minorities and the poor. Proponents of development, conversely, may oppose hazardous waste sites or shopping malls for fear of consequences to property values or their personal environment.

This theory implies that consensus is changing constantly. Support today for one policy or another can evaporate tomorrow. The electorate voted against growth management in the late 1970s and early 1980s but now favors managing (if not stopping) growth, at least in many jurisdictions. The waning of conservation priorities on the federal level during the Reagan era was balanced by an unprecedented activism by the states on behalf of land conservation. But the conflict of dual capitalist principles, as Plotkin describes, continues. A future famine or political upheaval, or even less dramatic stimuli, will inevitably alter the balance of conservation politics again.

A different theory has been gaining attention lately. Some conservation organizations have recently been professing biblical proscriptions for a religious ethic of stewardship. A. S. Mather, a geographer at the University of Aberdeen has articulated this dialectical theory of land use conflicts tied to competing biblical messages. One views land as a commodity to be used and exploited to man's benefit; the other sees land as a heritage over which man has stewardship responsibilities but no absolute right of disposal or exclusive ownership.

Many theories are professed to explain the motives and rationale for use of land. From the ideological to the purely utilitarian, many of them have some justification. To be effective, formulation of policy needs to account for the various motivations of private landowners and managers. But land management decisions are not necessarily rational.

Urban growth and land use in modern times are typically discontinuous and haphazard. Urban growth has tended to proceed as small, individual parcels become available largely as a result of community economic conditions and/or the financial status of individual owners. In other words, government policy has not been the dominant influence on land use patterns. Furthermore, different developers are responsible for different kinds of development as well as different parcels. Neither is development continuous over time. Just as there are booms and busts in economic growth, there are bursts and slowdowns in land development that result in odd patterns of land use. Thus, overall patterns are often products of numerous, separate, and unconnected decisions.

Since land use patterns are essentially determined by private economic objectives, theoretically, government efforts to direct land use needs to be designed with an understanding of private rationale for land use decisions. Given the disjointed nature of private decision making, however, it is difficult for policymakers to design policy that will provide effective incentives for public land use goals. Landowners may make management decisions that are contrary to their own interests and may directly contradict their stated land use goals. There are many reasons to explain such phenomena. A simple explanation proffered by Mather, in reference to farm management, is that

> because of the tendency to make habitual decisions and to conform to a group of which [the landowner] is a member, it is not surprising that a land use may persist long after the conditions under which it was first selected have ceased to operate. Inertia is probably as common in choice of land use as it is in other realms of human activity.[3]

Predicting future land use patterns is similar to predicting the economy. The justification for a particular policy adopted today may not be present later when demographics and/or the economy changes. Farmers and other landowners frequently persist in managing land in ways that were justified when circumstances were much different than they are in the present. Government policy, also, reflects outdated conditions of land value and utility.

Land use decisions and public policy arise from a complex interaction and combination of many factors and conditions. According to Professor Frank Popper of Rutgers University,

> the American federalist system of land use controls ... is so loose, so deliberately disjointed and open-ended, that it is barely a system in the sense that European elite civil service bureaucracies understand the term. The right to make particular regulatory decisions shifts unpredictably over time from one level of government to another. No principle of administrative rationality, constitutional entitlement, economic efficiency, or even ideological predisposition truly determines the governmental locus of decisions. It is more often a matter of the inevitably uncertain catch-as-catch-can pluralism of democratic power politics.[4]

Political pendulums are indeed inherent in the democratic process. But the recent trend in the states (under both conservative and liberal administrations) has been one of increasing centralization of land use management. And this trend is directly related to population growth and urbanization of society. Some experts suggest that this centralization of land use policy originated in Britain with the passage of the Town and Country Planning Act in 1947.

Ideas such as this have crossed the ocean, and states have begun to exercise greater autonomy on a variety of land use matters. Their land conservation and management policies fall into three categories (regulation, incentive programs, and land acquisition and management). This book discusses some of the specific programs and policies adopted by different states and some issues raised about the new state activism in land regulation. It provides the latest information available on the number of states that have adopted certain policies, summarizes the elements of programs of particular interest, and describes recent trends in growth management initiatives. It does not attempt to provide detailed policy analyses, although the literature cited and bibliography are good starting points. This is intended to be a useful primer on state land conservation policy. Limitations of space, time, and budget require that the complexity and controversy of evaluation are left to others.

II

History of Land Policy

City and town planning has an ancient history. Many European old cities were originally laid out by their feudal lords (or their generals) with designs to enhance defense. Early American city plats were likewise drawn for defensive objectives and for ease of providing public services.

Modern urban land use regulation in America began shortly after the turn of the century. Los Angeles initiated municipal land use regulations in 1909 with rudimentary zoning of residential and industrial uses. New York was the first city to adopt a comprehensive zoning code in 1910. Within 10 years, over 420 cities had followed suit.

There is ample precedent for government regulation of rural land as well. Historically, governments have intervened in agricultural markets on grounds of national defense, foreign trade, and social stability. Modern land conservation and regulation has its antecedents in royal protection of forests for ships' timbers and wildlife hunting. Periods of more or less government involvement in agricultural production have cycled, and total acreage devoted to crop production has expanded or contracted, having significant effect on land values as well as land use.

Land generally has economic value only if it is used for some kind of utilitarian purpose, such as food production, dwelling, manufacturing, or commercial trade. Only recently has land been given financial value for purely passive use or for its intrinsic value, such as for wildlife habitat or species preservation. Even its intrinsic values may not be recognized by the public unless some development or human alteration occurs, such as the addition of picnic tables or construction of a nature interpretation center. Only relatively recently has man been putting a dollar value on some lands for their nonutilitarian values.

Historically, land alone has had little economic value unless an "improvement" was added. As defined by tax codes and by real estate professionals, improvement means a structure is on the land. The ability to inflate the economic value of land by building a structure or otherwise altering the land invites speculation as well as investment. Public policies to encourage investment, and therefore speculation, have a longer history and take up more space in the code books than conservation policies.

Land speculation has a deep tradition in America. The personal wealth of some of our founding fathers, including George Washington and Ben Franklin, was largely created through land speculation. Some of our early leaders even used their political offices for vast personal gain. They would not survive under today's political standards.

But then throughout most of American history, public policy, reflecting the public's temperament, was one of development. Settling the western frontier was the nation's social priority. The U.S. government itself acted as a broker in what we today would consider land speculation, setting the tone for development by selling large tracks of land at a profit beginning with the Ordinance of 1785 and other acts.

At the very least, speculation was tacit public policy, and abuse of land resources under these policies was tolerated if not encouraged. As described by Peter Wolf in his book, *Land in America: Its Value, Use and Control:*

> While the pioneer is portrayed in film and lore as a courageous adventurer, more often flamboyant and carefree than conservative and circumspect, there were other types on the frontier as well. Many of the westward-moving pioneers became land speculators or their agents. It took capital to become a speculator, however, and most settlers hoped to profit in one way or another by controlling an extra quarter-section, which they would sell when demand was high.[5]

Huge wealth was possible for the first land speculator in one of the many towns that popped up on the frontier. Fraudulent land deals started long before Florida swamp sales at the turn of the century, and speculation was inevitably a part of a new nation's growth across the continent. Spurring that growth was official policy, and the political establishment found the amount of corruption and fraud inherent in that great demographic and social movement tolerable.

The federal government granted more than 130 million acres to railroads during the last half of the 19th century in exchange, basically, for making large-scale settlement of the West possible. In the granting of such vast lands to the railroads and the subsequent settlement of two-thirds of the nation, Wolf sees the convention of development-without-planning being firmly established in political tradition:

> In the laying out and building of regional and transcontinental railroads, there was no attempt to plan the overall scheme of the rail lines themselves, their points of link, interchange, or territory of coverage.... Nor was any national philosophy adopted ... regarding the orderly development of communities in relationship to one another, or even in the orderly development of individual communities.... Thus, the first lands to be opened and exploited were always of apparent richness, those that were fertile or suitable for easy clearing. Afterwards, the migratory, land-wise early settlers moved on down the line, often to the edge of the frontier, to prepare for another round of settlement.
>
> This approach to the land, and pattern of development, can be seen in the placement of communities across America today. Moreover, it continues to be the way in which land is exploited in each region, around each metropolitan area, indeed in each community. The specter of suburban sprawl in the major metropolitan zones of the country shows a continuation of this leaping outward to the best land, ignoring poorer lands along the way, as the highways of mid-twentieth century, like the railroads before them, moved out into the countryside often ahead of all settlement, and almost always without a well-conceived plan that linked the most desirable patterns of settlement to the provision of access.[6]

The imperative of 19th century America, after all, was not orderly development but development, period. Now that the West has been won and the nation essentially settled, the public's priority of interest is turning from development to preservation of its natural heritage and maintenance of a high quality of life. Planning and conservation are gaining respectability and greater political power.

The primary vehicle of states' exercise of land use authority has been in zoning. Zoning is a police power which has been delegated to local government by the states. After initial adoption by Los Angeles and New York shortly after the turn of the century, Herbert Hoover, who was secretary of commerce at the time, directed the preparation of the Standard State Zoning Enabling Act in 1924. All states now have zoning statutes modeled after this standard. Zoning has been the primary and most significant land law in the nation ever since. New powers are being exercised by the states, and a new body of land law is being created. Whether zoning will remain the predominant method of land regulation in the future is unknown.

But zoning and the states' police power behind it are not necessarily the primary approach for the future. American public policy until the middle of this century has primarily been to encourage land speculation and development. In essence, we are in a period of reevaluation and reformulation of land policies. According to Hite, Wolf, Mathers, and others, current land policy is based on past conditions that may have been appropriate at the time. We have not yet created a policy structure that meets today's imperatives, but we are in the process of doing so. In the words of Hite:

> A strong case can be made that even with all its faults, even with all the opportunities it presented for graft and corruption, permitting land speculators to act as catalysts for the settlement of the continent was, on balance, a wise course of action. In fostering land speculation on the frontier, the nation established a tradition that has long outlived whatever usefulness it had. Land speculation became a great game to Americans; they became addicted to it in the way that some men become compulsive gamblers. Yet the tradition did not die; the game went on and on, creating economic waste and needless environmental destruction.
>
> .... Land speculation is a mass participation game with millions of players from all strata of American life. Even those not actively involved in the game are apt to oppose any measures which might impede their participation at some later date. There is no more reason to be optimistic that land speculation can be wiped out in America than to believe that alcoholism, prostitution, and thievery can be wiped out. Yet if effective land-use policies and programs are to be established, land speculation must be

> refocused. The game must be played under a new, modified set of rules. The rules of the great American game are implicitly determined by the laws of property, the operations of the market, and the incidence of taxation.[7]

Zoning, regulation, public management, and other measures are still the primary lexicon in public land policy. The next chapter describes their tradition and legality and then discusses recent trends in land management.

III

State Powers and Case Law

During the pioneering of America, liberals and conservatives alike and the dominant political parties at any given time all shared a conviction that land development was a priority. One of the sociocultural ethics behind this consensus was (and remains) the conviction that every citizen has the right to pursue property ownership and, therefore, economic parity. In modern times, this philosophy is embodied in homeownership, a house with a yard and a garage in the suburbs. In Wolf's words,

> It was argued by even the most ardent land reformers that the landholder must be given the absolute right to sell, mortgage, or lease his land for any purpose whatsoever, and to anyone. Fewer rights would constitute a sham, a commitment of a republican government to unfree tenure and the notions of feudalism. Until around 1880, most private owners and public officials concurred that unfettered, unlimited rights associated with private ownership of land would bring political stability and national prosperity. Through the use of the land—broadly distributed and owned without restriction and control—the country was expected to realize its democratic purpose and promise, in contrast to the class-dominated nations of Europe. Total freedom in the private use of land was thus equated with individualism and liberty.[8]

With this philosophical heritage as a backdrop, it is easy to understand how any government efforts to restrict or slow development result in controversy. Regulation raises questions fundamental to Americans' perception of their social order. It also frequently brings up tangible constitutional issues.

Land law in America is determined as often in the courts as in the legislatures. American as well as British common law traces private property rights back to the Magna Charta when English nobles forced King John in 1215 A.D. to recognize property rights. English jurisprudence since then has recognized property as "the third absolute right" of every citizen. Subsequently, the American Bill of Rights included wording reminiscent of English law: "No person shall ... be deprived of life, liberty, or property, without due process of law; nor shall private property be taken for public use, without a just compensation." This dictum has provided the points of argument for most challenges to state authority over land use policy.

But the U.S. Constitution includes another explicit clause regarding state powers and authority that carries equal if not preeminent weight in legal arguments: "The powers not delegated to the United States by the Constitution, nor prohibited by it to the states, are reserved to the states respectively, or to the people." Eventually, this clause of the Constitution, the Tenth Amendment, was interpreted to mean that the states were delegated the authority of self-government. The term *police power* refers to states' power to act in the public interest. Common law has now firmly established the authority of states to regulate private property as long as it is "in the public interest." What constitutes the public interest is also largely found in case law. Absolute rights of private landowners, therefore, are abridged by the principle that the public interest is superior to private property rights.

John Stuart Mill, a 19th century economist with ample free market credentials wrote in his tome, *Principles of Political Economy,* that

> the claim of the landowners to the land is altogether subordinate to the general policy of the state. The principle of property gives them no right to the land, but only a right to compensation for whatever portion of their interest in the land it may be the policy of the state to deprive them of.[9]

One of the first cases that helped establish this principle was a lower court ruling in 1831 in which a Boston court upheld the authority of local government to regulate the use of private property even if compensation for loss of some rights is not made. The

U.S. Supreme Court first endorsed this concept in *Mugler v. Kansas* in 1887 when it held that the exercise of police power over private property, even if destructive of that property, is not the same as a taking without due process or compensation.[10]

In one interpretation of the concept of police power (*Berman v. Parker,* 1954), the Supreme Court said that

> an attempt to define its reach or trace its outer limits is fruitless, for each case must turn on its own facts. The definition is essentially the product of legislative determinations addressed to the purposes of government, purposes neither abstractly nor historically capable of complete definition. Subject to specific constitutional limitations, when the legislature has spoken, the public interest has been declared in terms well-not conclusive....[11]

State legislatures, then, have broad powers to define the public interest or public welfare. As states have exercised more of their inherent authority in environmental policy, legislatures have defined environmental quality as an express public interest in statutory statements. This definition of environmental quality as a legitimate public interest has been upheld by the courts. For example, a Florida appellate court ruled in 1977 (*Moviematic Industries Corp. v. Board of County Commissioners of Metropolitan Dade County*) that

> we find the inclusion of ecological considerations as a legitimate objective of zoning ordinances and resolutions is long overdue and hold that preservation of the ecological balance of a particular area is a valid exercise of the police power....[12]

In *Graham v. Estuary Properties* (1981), the Florida Supreme Court, whose ruling was later upheld by the U.S. Supreme Court, stated that "protection of environmentally sensitive areas and pollution prevention are legitimate concerns within the police power."[13] The Wisconsin Supreme Court similarly ruled in *Just v. Marinette County* that

> an owner of land has no absolute and unlimited right to change the essential natural character of his land so as to use it for a purpose for which it was unsuited in its natural state and which injures the rights of others. The exercise of police power in zoning must be reasonable and we think it is not unreasonable exercise of that power to prevent harm to public rights by limiting the use of private property to its natural uses.[14]

The first major challenge to zoning law came in *Village of Euclid v. Ambler Realty Company* when in 1926 the Supreme Court ruled that zoning was a legal extension of a government's police power and constitutional unless its provisions were clearly arbitrary and unreasonable, having no substantial relation to the public health, safety, morals, or general welfare.[15]

In recent years, states' land use policies have been challenged on the grounds that they constitute a taking without compensation. These challenges find their precedence in a 1922 case in which Justice Oliver Wendell Holmes wrote the Court's opinion and said, in part:

> Government hardly could go on if to some extent values incident to property could not be diminished without paying for every such change in the general law. As long recognized, some values are enjoyed under an implied limitation and must yield to the police power. But obviously the implied limitation must have its limits or the contract and due process clauses are gone. One fact for consideration in determining such limits is the extent of diminution. When it reaches a certain magnitude, in most if not in all cases there must be an exercise of eminent domain and compensation to sustain the act. So the question depends upon the particular facts.
>
> .... We are in danger of forgetting that a strong public desire to improve the public condition is not enough to warrant achieving the desire by a shorter cut than the constitutional way of paying for the change.
>
> .... The general rule at least is, that while property may be regulated to a certain extent, if regulation goes too far it will be recognized as a taking.[16]

Subsequently, most serious challenges to government regulation of land use have turned on this question. In a series of cases, then, the courts have been establishing the boundaries of legitimate government authority to regulate land use for environmental conservation purposes and legitimate private property rights. But fundamentally, the question is always open with each case subject to interpretation of its facts.

The body of law that is emerging suggests that government regulatory actions can result in significant diminution of private property values without constituting a taking. Regulation that allows some economic return, that is clearly in the public interest and that clearly is not arbitrary or capricious, has a likelihood of meeting court tests. One means by which governments have successfully defended land use and conservation policies before the courts has been to develop comprehensive plans upon which zoning and other land use policies are then based. The trend toward more comprehensive planning by both states and local governments has been fed by the increase of challenges to land management and conservation authorities.

Note: For an exhaustive discussion of constitutional and case law on land use policy, *see* "Wetland Regulation," by Richard Hamann in *4 Rohan, Zoning and Land Use Controls;* Williams' and Taylor's *American Planning Law: Land Use and the Police Power;* and Wolf's *Land in America: Its Value, Use and Control.*

IV

Generic Land Use and Conservation Programs

In the past two decades, states have dramatically expanded their role in land use policy beyond just enabling zoning authorities. From resource management and conservation to economic development and capital planning, states are exercising reserved authorities in land policy in many ways.

During the 1970s, a number of states adopted environmental and resource management performance standards, which led to debates on extensive growth control legislation and direct land use regulations. Political consensus changed, however, and only a few states such as Oregon, Vermont, and Florida embarked on the path of integrated, comprehensive land use planning. But state land use policymaking did not slow down. Rather, it shifted focus to specific issues of land use such as wetlands, farmland, critical areas, floodplain development, and waste facility and industrial siting.

In a widely heralded article on land use policy, Popper, chairman of the Urban Studies Department at Rutgers, said that state land use policy is more centralized now than ever before but more likely to be specialized and oriented to particular purposes. This chapter describes some of the main elements of these specialized policies and the states that have enacted them.

Wetlands Preservation

Wetlands are ecological transition zones between aquatic and terrestrial systems. They are often cited as being the most productive ecosystems, "more biologically productive than an Iowa corn field." Sportsmen have always recognized the value of wetlands as habitat for fish and wildlife. Only recently has the general public come to realize the importance of wetland ecosystems for environmental quality. Monetary values are being ascribed to wetlands for their role in pollution control, flood abatement, groundwater recharge, and erosion control.

It is estimated that more than half of the original wetlands present when the pilgrims landed have been destroyed by farming and development. Some species of wildlife, including popular game animals, are fast being depleted. The U.S. Fish and Wildlife Service fears that several duck species, for example, may become endangered.

Wetlands regulations are becoming more politically feasible. President Bush made the protection of wetlands a priority issue in his 1988 campaign. A number of states have begun to regulate land uses and activities that destroy wetlands and to acquire them for recreation and conservation. Virtually all coastal states have some form of shoreline land use restrictions, usually under floodplain protection or coastal zone management authorities. At least 17 states* have laws intended to protect inland wetlands from conversion to other uses.[17]

Wetlands preservation statutes vary in composition from state to state. No two statutes are alike, but taken as a composite, a model can be derived from the individual components of all these state programs. Such a model would include:

(1) Explicit statement of goals;
(2) Inventory and mapping of wetlands;
(3) Precise technical definition of wetlands;
(4) Wetlands classifications scheme;
(5) Delineation of permitting authority and jurisdiction;
(6) Planning and permitting criteria;
(7) Enforcement procedures (including appeals and penalties);
(8) Mitigation and restoration system (such as wetlands "banks");

* California, Connecticut, Florida, Maine, Massachusetts, Minnesota, Michigan, Maryland, Nebraska, New Hampshire, New Jersey, New York, North Dakota, Oregon, Rhode Island, Virginia, and Wisconsin.

(9) Coordination and cooperation among private and multiple public sector entities;
(10) Tax incentives for preservation;
(11) Research and education programs; and
(12) Authorization and appropriations for acquisition of fee simple title or conservation easements of valuable wetlands.

Examples of statutory language for wetlands protection policies can be found in various state laws. New Jersey law provides a statement of goals, for example, that reads: "It shall be the policy of the state to preserve the purity and integrity of freshwater wetlands from random, unnecessary, or undesirable alteration or disturbance."

Mapping is key to a state's effective enforcement of its permitting authority to regulate destruction of wetlands. By 1977, New York's Department of Environmental Conservation had mapped all wetlands of 12.5 acres or larger. This enabled state and local authorities to identify landowners and administer the permit program for regulating wetlands alteration under the wetlands protection act adopted in 1975. The department is the authorized permitting agency in New York, although local governments have the option of assuming this function. In Florida, the Department of Environmental Regulation shares permitting authority with regional Water Management Districts, depending on the land use classification.

Mitigation of destructive activities in wetlands is one way that states achieve a so-called no net loss of these resources. Wetlands banking is a form of mitigation used by Minnesota, New Jersey, and North Dakota. Wetlands can be deposited in the "bank" by conservation groups, donated by private landowners, directly purchased by state agencies, or set aside when an "artificial" wetland is created by highway construction or other means and lies on public right of way or other public land. When a permit is issued for drainage or filling of a wetland, then a "withdrawal" from the bank is processed. As in North Dakota, if the assets held in the bank fall below a certain level, permits for wetlands alteration are suspended. Developers or farmers may obtain permits conditioned on making a deposit to the wetlands bank in cash or acres equivalent to or greater than the wetlands acreage being destroyed. Free market proponents are attracted to this concept because it avoids outright prohibition of altering wetlands and creates an auxiliary "market" for use in their natural condition.

Intergovernmental and intragovernmental coordination and cooperation are important if agencies with different responsibilities are to work together effectively to protect wetlands. Some states, such as Florida, allow local governments to enforce their own wetlands permitting authorities. Other states preempt local governments from regulating wetlands. Michigan is the only state that has assumed authority from the federal government to enforce Section 404 permits under the Clean Water Act, although New Jersey wrote its wetlands act with the specific objective of assuming this authority. Section 404 is the authority for federal regulation of draining and filling activities in wetlands. Several states share Section 404 responsibilities with the U.S. Army Corps of Engineers and the Environmental Protection Agency.

Some states have tax incentives to encourage private conservation of wetlands. Minnesota, for example, exempts all wetlands from property taxes.

Virtually all states could acquire wetlands for conservation purposes, but many have explicit language for this purpose in their wetlands regulatory statutes. Funding for land acquisition spans a variety of sources. Sales taxes, real estate transfer fees, severance taxes, luxury taxes, gasoline taxes, lotteries, fees and licenses, and bond issues are some of these sources.

Agricultural Land Preservation

For a few years in the late 1970s and early 1980s, land conservation was almost synonymous with agricultural land preservation. Farmland protection was a fairly popular issue when broader conservation and environmental issues were not. Surveys by Nancy Bushwick Malloy at the National Association of State Departments of Agriculture during the 1980s showed remarkable growth in the number of preservation programs. As reported in NASDA's *Farmland Notes,* by 1987 every state had adopted differential property taxation on agricultural land.[18]

In addition, 47 states had passed right-to-farm language. *Right-to-farm policies* usually protect farm operators from nuisance suits and/or local regulations that place restrictions on conventional agricultural practices. Nuisance suits typically result when subdivisions replace farmland and the remaining farmers become targets of complaints by new residents for smells and other "undesirable" activities that are part of normal farming. Nevada, South Dakota, and Wyoming were the only states that had no right-to-farm policies when last surveyed in 1986.

Fewer states had experimented with more complex programs such as agricultural districting, zoning, and transfers of development rights (TDRs). *Transfer of development rights* is any mechanism for separating rights to develop the property from fee simple ownership and allowing more intensive development elsewhere. Frequently, this approach is part of agricultural districting and includes a provision for financial penalties if the property is ever developed for nonagricultural purposes. Fourteen states have some kind of provision for purchasing or transferring development rights from farmland.* Twelve states have agricultural districting programs.** Twenty-eight states have enabled or authorized state agencies or local governments to establish agricultural use zones in land use zoning regulations.†

Finally, a number of governors have issued executive orders to state agencies to adopt farmland protection as a primary objective in carrying out their administrative duties. The significance of executive orders lies in the degree of farmland conversion that results from state projects and programs as diverse as highway construction and financing of government operations. Fifteen states have executive orders.‡

One of the first states to adopt a farmland protection policy was California under its Land Conservation (Williamson) Act of 1965. The act authorizes 10-year contractual agreements among local governments and farm operators to create "agricultural preserves." Land under contract is assessed at its value for farming and protected by right-to-farm measures.

Wisconsin provides tax credits to farmers whose land is included within a local agricultural zone and is covered by an agricultural preservation plan.

States that have adopted growth management statutes have done so, in part, on the grounds of protecting agricultural land from development. Oregon, Vermont, and Hawaii were the first states to pass statewide agricultural protection programs that became comprehensive growth management strategies. Other states that have followed their lead are Delaware, Florida, Georgia, Maine, New Jersey, and Rhode Island. These programs are discussed in more detail in chapter six.

*Connecticut, Florida, Maryland, Massachusetts, New Hampshire, New Jersey, New York, North Carolina, Pennsylvania, Rhode Island, Vermont, Virginia, Washington, and West Virginia.

**California, Illinois, Iowa, Kentucky, Maryland, Minnesota, New Jersey, New York, North Carolina, Ohio, Pennsylvania, and Virginia.

† California, Colorado, Delaware, Florida, Hawaii, Idaho, Illinois, Indiana, Iowa, Kansas, Maine, Maryland, Michigan, Minnesota, Nebraska, New Hampshire, New Jersey, New York, North Dakota, Oregon, Pennsylvania, South Dakota, Utah, Vermont, Virginia, Washington, Wisconsin, and Wyoming.

‡ Connecticut, Delaware, Georgia, Illinois, Kentucky, Maryland, Massachusetts, Michigan, Minnesota, North Carolina, Ohio, Pennsylvania, Vermont, Virginia, and Washington.

Conservation Easements

With the decline of federal assistance for the purchase of park and conservation lands, states began to seek not only alternative funds for acquisition but also concepts to achieve conservation objectives short of outright ownership. The idea of separating rights to develop land from other ownership rights had been tested by several states' agricultural land preservation policies, i.e., transferable development rights (see section on agricultural land preservation). Private exchanges of easements have a fairly well-developed history for purposes such as transportation, preservation of historic sites or artifacts, and utility transmission. The extension of easement ownership to purposes of conservation was, therefore, not an exaggerated leap in real estate law.

As defined in *The Conservation Easement Handbook* (by the Trust for Public Lands and the Land Trust Exchange), a *conservation easement* is

> a legal agreement a property owner makes to restrict the type and amount of development that may take place on his or her property. Each easement's restrictions are tailored to the particular property and to the interests of the individual owner.[19]

Fifteen states and the District of Columbia* have adopted the Uniform Conservation Easement Act developed by the National Conference of Commissioners on Uniform State Laws.[20] The rationale behind state conservation easement acts is primarily to encourage private donations of easements to local land trusts or nature conservancies through tax benefits. These statutes also enable government entities to purchase, receive, and administer lands under conservation easement.

Codification of conservation easement rules also provides additional protection from civil challenges to deed restrictions. It is an assumption by the authors of these acts that land use restrictions or "affirmative duties" are binding upon the successors or assigns of the original parties. There are some legal scholars who argue that such protection is, in reality, minimal, depending on the specific wording of a given statute.

The term *easement* has been used in these statutes because it is legally more comprehensive, more defensible against common

* Alaska, Arizona, Arkansas, Idaho, Indiana, Kentucky, Maine, Minnesota, Mississippi, Nevada, Oregon, South Dakota, Texas, Virginia, Wisconsin, and the District of Columbia.

law challenges, and more flexible than legal alternatives such as covenants or servitudes.

Conservation easements are being used to protect wetlands and other biological resources, establish outdoor recreation and parks such as the Appalachian Trail, preserve farmland for farmland use, maintain scenic vistas such as mountain tops and river shorelines, and preserve archaeological or historic sites. Recreation access on private lands is becoming a significant interest of groups that represent outdoor recreationists such as sportsmen, rafters, hikers, and bird watchers.

Wildlife Management Incentives

Wildlife management on the state level has primarily been a function of voluntary cooperation among private landowners, sportsmen, and state game and fish agencies. Land management techniques applied to habitat are the principal means of wildlife conservation in addition to regulation of harvesting through hunting and fishing licenses and setting of seasons. The largest source of funding for state wildlife conservation is hunting and fishing licenses.

As demand for outdoor recreation has increased simultaneously with declines in acreage open to hunting, states have begun to take a more proactive role in encouraging wildlife habitat conservation by private landowners, especially farmers. During the farm crisis of the mid-1980s, many farmers asked for state assistance to diversify their operations and develop alternative markets to improve overall net revenues from farmland. At the same time, the 1985 farm bill was written with emphasis on reducing farm commodity surpluses by creation of the Conservation Reserve Program and sodbuster and swampbuster provisions to increase set-aside farmland. Conservationists viewed these set-aside programs as important opportunities for wildlife conservation. States simultaneously began to investigate these wildlife resources as potential revenue opportunities for farmers.

In a 1986 survey of states, the Montana Department of Fish, Wildlife, and Parks found that twenty-six states* had programs designed to foster land conservation for wildlife management ob-

* Alabama, California, Colorado, Connecticut, Illinois, Indiana, Iowa, Louisiana, Maryland, Michigan, Montana, Nebraska, New Hampshire, New Mexico, New York, North Carolina, North Dakota, Ohio, Oklahoma, Oregon, Pennsylvania, South Carolina, Tennessee, Washington, Wisconsin, and Wyoming.

jectives.[21] These programs are of several types. Usually administered by fish and wildlife agencies, they may include tax benefits, state management of habitat, lease payments, payments for game damage and/or fee payments to owners collected by the state. Some state programs provide limited protection of landowners from liability exposure. Liability is the single most important reason landowners cite for not allowing hunting/fishing access, which is the critical justification for wildlife management.

Land Acquisition for Parks and Natural Areas

Collectively, states administer about 10 million acres as state parks. This acreage represents about 10 percent of all public parkland—federal, state, and local. The states own another 40 million acres of forests and wildlife management areas. Since a variety of state agencies administer these lands, no single source of information on their management status or condition exists. The individual states themselves frequently have inadequate information on their properties. Nevertheless, these lands represent a major national conservation effort that continues to grow.

Outright acquisition of land for parks and for preservation of sensitive areas is perhaps the oldest way that states have achieved land conservation. Again, loss of federal financial aid for conservation purposes at first reduced states' programs significantly, but constituents' demands for outdoor recreation and land conservation created political support for state initiatives. The result was a number of state innovations to fund land acquisition. Surveys by the National Park Service, the National Recreation and Park Association, and the Nature Conservancy illustrate at least 17 methods of funding land conservation in addition to general appropriations:

(1) Severance taxes: Florida, Louisiana, Michigan, Montana, New Mexico, Tennessee, and Wisconsin.
(2) Real estate transfer fees: Florida, Maryland, Vermont.
(3) Cigarette taxes: Nebraska, New Mexico, Texas.
(4) Hotel/motel room surcharges: West Virginia.
(5) Sales taxes: Missouri.
(6) Gasoline taxes: Arizona, California, Idaho, Maine, Minnesota, Montana, New Mexico, Ohio, South Dakota, Washington, and Wyoming.
(7) Lotteries: Colorado and Iowa.

(8) Charitable gambling: North Dakota.
(9) Boat licenses: Arizona, Minnesota, New York, Ohio, Pennsylvania, South Carolina, and Virginia.
(10) All-terrain vehicle taxes: California, Idaho, Minnesota, and Ohio.
(11) Snowmobile taxes: Idaho, Indiana, Minnesota, New York, Ohio, Pennsylvania, and South Dakota.
(12) Parks entry fees: Iowa and Pennsylvania.
(13) Hunting and fishing licenses: Indiana, New Jersey, South Carolina, and Virginia.
(14) Donations from foundations: California, Colorado, Minnesota, and South Dakota.
(15) Income tax refund checkoffs: Indiana, New Jersey, Ohio, Oklahoma, Pennsylvania, Virginia, and West Virginia.
(16) Bond issues: Florida, Minnesota, New Jersey, Pennsylvania, and Washington.
(17) Endowments or trust funds: Iowa and Minnesota (pending in Nevada).

Most of the enabling legislation or ballot initiatives for these funds were passed in the 1980s. Usually for multiyear periods, funding levels range from half a million dollars to $785 million (for a bond measure passed in 1988 in California). Many states with smaller funding levels have already increased them. Much of this new-found funding will not be available for a few years, but it appears to foreshadow a dramatic increase in state parkland acreage and conservation programs.

Other Authorities

Several other state land regulatory policies affect land conservation. Probably most notable are the various Coastal Zone Management Programs adopted by coastal states pursuant to the federal Coastal Zone Management Act of 1972. Frequently cited as a precursor to statewide growth management policies, this act provided a model for debates during the 1970s over proposals for a national land use policy.

Most coastal states have approved costal zone management acts. The exceptions, according to the Coastal States Organization, are Georgia, Illinois, Indiana, Minnesota, Ohio, and Texas. The latter two, however, are in the process of developing their programs and are seeking approval from the Office of Coastal Zone Management within the National Oceanic and Atmospheric Administration of the Department of Commerce. Approval hinges on a state's adopting land use regulations within a defined area of the coastal zone. In return, the federal government provides funding assistance for planning, conservation, and mitigating impacts of energy developments. Another incentive for developing a program is the potential for a state to assume U.S. Army Corps of Engineers' authority to administer Section 404 dredge and fill permits in wetlands.

The flood insurance program of the Federal Emergency Management Agency is another federal program that requires state and local government enforcement of certain land use regulations that may affect conservation. For property owners to qualify for federally subsidized flood insurance, their local government must have certified floodplain development regulations. The objective of floodplain regulations is to minimize development of floodplains, which results in billions of dollars of costs to the taxpayer when floods do occur. Local governments, of course, must have enabling language in their states' codes to enact these regulations. All states now have enabled such local government action. A few have gone further by reviewing local permit activities and/or establishing special programs for specific floodplains. Virtually every state provides technical support to local governments in their floodplain management programs.

Many states have various performance standards for specific land use activities that are intended to conserve the resource. Fifteen states have forest practice acts that define certain standards of timber harvesting to ensure regeneration and minimize water pollution. California's, Oregon's, and Washington's are probably the three most controversial acts insofar as they have strict performance standards in an attempt to control soil erosion from steep hillsides of the commercially valuable forests of the Northwest.

Forest practice acts and soil conservation programs identify best management practices in agriculture and forestry. They are not "land conservation" programs as much as "resource conservation" policies, but they do represent the states' legislative expressions of concern about land use practices.

A variety of facility siting statutes have been passed in recent years. They have been adopted both to limit the power of local opponents in blocking siting of essential public services as well as private economic enterprises and to ensure that environmental quality is recognized as an explicit criteria in the site selection process. To the extent that they succeed in avoiding inappropriate development of sensitive lands, they constitute an effective land conservation objective. Such statutes are frequently written, however, in the context of how a particular development should be located rather than how a particular kind of land resource should be managed. Such laws have been passed for energy-generating facilities, solid and hazardous waste sites, industrial projects of various kinds, and several kinds of socially provocative institutions (X-rated theatres, adult bookstores, halfway houses, for example).

Groundwater contamination is a growing issue in most states. At least 37 states have adopted some statutory policy to protect groundwater from excessive contamination levels. Most of these statutes address specific sources of contamination by requiring that certain design standards be met or by regulating polluting activities through discharge permits. A handful of states (Connecticut, Minnesota, New York, Rhode Island, and Washington) have enacted land use management regulations to minimize land activities in aquifer recharge zones. For example, New York's groundwater protection statute specifically authorizes the use of upzoning for the purpose of protecting areas of critical recharge.

Summary

A number of other state regulatory policies affect land use or resources. They include mined land reclamation, soil conservation, and a variety of performance standards applicable to land development activities. This chapter has presented the most significant policies for which detailed information was readily at hand.

Regulating Sensitive Lands by Jon Kusler provides a more comprehensive, detailed review of state regulation of sensitive areas. It discusses why certain areas are considered sensitive and how they can be conserved through state regulation.

As the list of state land conservation measures illustrates, centralized land use management continues to expand. According to Popper,

> Its fortunes ebb and flow, depending mainly on the politics of individual states, federal agencies, or land use fields.... Its unfamiliarity has diminished, and it is becoming utterly acceptable, even ordinary, to much of the political spectrum, including many of its former enemies.[22]

Citing New Jersey's statutes on wetlands, hazardous waste, coastal zone management, farmland protection, affordable housing, and critical areas protection, Popper said that in combination these separate statutes may be as effective as integrated state land use programs. New Jersey, in fact, is one of the states that has adopted state land use planning and consolidated political support for land conservation and comprehensive planning. Growth management has indeed received new support, and more states are considering this path to land management policy.

V

Critical Areas Programs

In a few of the larger states with population pressures in areas of critical resource values, legislation has been adopted that attempts to conserve land resources while still meeting economic needs of residents. These states have created regional land use management agencies explicitly authorized to cooperate with local and federal jurisdictions in administering their respective programs. Easements, land use regulations, economic development initiatives, air and water quality regulations, industrial siting procedures, and resource management performance standards are some of the tools these agencies use to achieve conservation objectives.

New York established the first critical areas program with creation of the Adirondack State Park. New Jersey's Pinelands Reserve is probably the most widely cited example of this conservation strategy. Lake Tahoe Regional Development Authority is the only one that is constituted under an interstate, federally approved authority, although one may be proposed for the Chesapeake Bay region.

Adirondack State Park

The state of New York owns only 40 percent of the land within the "blue line" of the oldest American state park, Adirondack State

Park. First recognized as a park by the New York Legislature in 1894, the area constitutes what the National Parks and Conservation Association refers to as a *greenline park,* a combination of public and private land managed for recreation and preservation objectives. Private landowners, in fact, control the majority of the six million acres of land in the park.

The Adirondack Park Agency Act of 1973 authorizes the Adirondack Park Agency (APA) to manage the state's lands, regulate certain uses within the private lands of the park, and cooperate with local governments and private landowners in the management of the rest of it.

The institution of the APA began with a state Senate Finance Committee report in 1966 that suggested that the park needed better management to accommodate visitors and the goal of conservation. The next year, Laurance Rockefeller commissioned a study calling for the creation of a national park for 1.7 million acres of the Adirondacks. The local response was vociferous and emphatic: NO.

Preservationists wanted Forever Wild status; hunters did not want game locked away; local governments feared loss of state revenues from the state forest preserve; townspeople saw a conspiracy of downstaters to lock land away for the rich. Conspiracy theories abounded.

Governor Nelson Rockefeller appointed the Temporary Study Commission on the Future of the Adirondacks. The commission had 10 members, but an advisory committee of 30 members was also appointed. Creation of the advisory committee guaranteed that essentially every issue would be aired and every interest heard.

In December 1970, the commission issued its recommendations: create the APA, classify state lands, subject towns' zoning proposals to the APA's review, develop master plans for both state and private lands, and issue bonds for acquiring scenic easements. Legislation enacting the recommendations was passed in June 1971.

The APA's first plans called for designating two million acres "Resource Management" (which required 42 acres for every principal building), 1.24 million acres as rural use (eight acres per building), 300,000 acres as low and moderate intensity use (3.2 and 1.3 acres per building, respectively), and 36,000 acres (mostly within town limits) for development. Development, even then, had to meet rigorous design standards. The APA's proposal was extensively amended by the legislature when it passed implementation bills in early 1973. Nevertheless, *Time* magazine was prompted to characterize it as "the most ambitious attempt ever to make development compatible with nature."

In recent years, the number of applications for developments within the park has increased about 60 percent a year. Widespread concern exists about the limits to the APA's authority. Consequently, Governor Mario Cuomo has appointed the Commission on the Adirondacks in the Twenty-First Century, which will make its recommendations for improved authority over the park in April 1990. The commission's crucial charge is to find solutions to chronic economic problems within the park's boundary while adequately conserving its natural and historic heritage.

Pinelands Reserve

The New Jersey Pinelands Protection Act of 1979 is similar to Oregon's Land Conservation and Development Act in that it explicitly attempts to ameliorate economic development conflicts with land resource conservation needs. The Pinelands act covers land use in only a portion of the state rather than throughout the state, although it extends to an area comprising a full fifth of New Jersey.

The one million acres of pine and oak forest that comprise the Pinelands overlie the Cohansey Aquifer, one of the state's primary sources of drinking water. The geology of the aquifer makes it particularly susceptible to contamination. Additionally, the region is essentially the last remaining area of wilderness in the highly developed, congested Middle Atlantic/Northeast urban corridor. These factors together with the anticipated growth of Atlantic City on the east and Philadelphia on the west convinced the legislature and Congress of the need to preserve the Pinelands but not at the expense of its communities' rural economy.

Congress designated the Pinelands the first national reserve under the National Parks and Recreation Act of 1978. New Jersey acted shortly thereafter with the Pinelands Protection Act to implement the federal goals. Thus, the Pinelands reserve represents cooperation among governments, agencies, and the public/private sectors to conserve a unique resource.

The state legislation created the Pinelands Commission and charged it with developing a comprehensive management plan to guide the region's land use. Adopted in 1980, the comprehensive plan designated 334,000 acres of the reserve as a preservation area district. Activities within this area are strictly regulated by the commission and local governments. Local governments are given much of the responsibility for implementing the act, but local plans and regulations must conform to the commission's comprehensive plan.

The Pinelands Commission may review and overrule any approval for development granted by local authorities.

Land uses considered to be appropriate in the preservation area include berry agriculture, forestry, recreation, limited resource extraction, and construction of necessary public infrastructure. Residential construction limits are 3.2 acre lots, and applicants for housing construction must demonstrate "a cultural, social, or economic link to the essential character of the Pinelands."

In addition to the preservation area district, there are four other land classification districts: forest, agricultural production, rural development, and regional growth areas, comprising 420,000, 79,000, 145,000, and 119,000 acres, respectively. The regional growth areas are similar in concept to the urban growth boundaries in Oregon's Land Conservation and Development Act.

Similarly, land uses are regulated to preserve forests and agriculture. Economic development is focused on the rural and regional development areas. Housing units are strictly limited. The Pinelands Protection Act, however, does not rely solely upon regulation of growth, it also incorporates transfers of development rights to redirect development voluntarily to the regional growth areas.

Lake Tahoe Regional Development Authority

Lake Tahoe is one of the few large, high-altitude lakes in the world. In addition to its unique and spectacular scenery, the ecology of the lake and surrounding areas is very sensitive. The lake is also convenient to large metropolitan populations on the West Coast. Its status as a famous recreational resort has led to extensive pressures for development.

The soils of the Lake Tahoe area are especially prone to erosion and sliding. Because it is a high-altitude "bowl," the area is vulnerable to air inversions and air pollution. The quality of the lake's water is degrading, and considering that Lake Tahoe is a mountain community, it is very congested from urbanization. Historically, the local population has resisted strong land use or environmental regulation. It has characterized lobbying for conservation or environmental policies as interference by outsiders.

In 1969, California, Nevada, and the U.S. Congress agreed on an interstate compact for the creation of the Tahoe Regional Planning Agency (TRPA). The agency developed and proposed a plan that would have reduced the rate of development, but as it was administered, the plan did not significantly reduce the pace of development. Critics faulted the structure of TRPA as the primary cause of its ineffectiveness. Prodevelopment interests, for example, usually succeeded in obtaining variances to the agency's most restrictive regulations.

Attempts to improve the authority of TRPA during the 1970s failed, in large part due to local officials' resentment of outside intervention in local affairs. The California attorney general filed suit to block two major casino projects, and the California Legislature reconstituted its Lake Tahoe management authority to form Cal-TRPA. Strict environmental design standards for development were imposed by the new agency. Simultaneously, California withdrew its funding for the old interstate TRPA, and California's representatives resigned.

In 1980, a new federal compact was ratified. The new TRPA has stronger environmental standards for both sides of the border, and the compact's authority gives the states greater control. Additionally, a nature conservancy in the Tahoe region is acquiring particularly sensitive lands for conservation purposes.

Other Examples of Critical Areas Programs

The Appalachian Trail is a national scenic trail extending from Georgia to Maine. Most of the trail is on private land but parts are in national forests, national parks, nature preserves, and state parks. Its management is performed under a series of cooperative agreements and easements among landowners; the National Park Service; and the Appalachian Mountain Club, the first private users' group to assume legal management authority and responsibility for a designated public right of use.

Special areas management has been proposed for a number of other places such as the Everglades ecosystem, Chesapeake Bay, Puget Sound, and smaller regional areas with critical environmental values. Despite the popularity of the concept of joint use/joint management land conservation, few examples of successful creation and administration of such areas exist. Nevertheless, the pluralistic, cooperative nature of their management plans suggests not only the reasons for their failure but also the source of their appeal. Having multiple interests involved in a conservation program increases the complexity of management but also broadens a sense of "ownership" of the "product."

Most sensitive areas span many ownerships and jurisdictional boundaries. Inevitably, there are fiscal and political limits to confiscatory policies. Therefore, interjurisdictional coordination and cooperation among multiple owners and managers are imperative if reasonable levels of conservation are to occur in large areas of environmental sensitivity. In many cases, there is no other political option.

VI

Comprehensive Growth Management Acts

In his presentation before the congressional Subcommittee on General Oversight and Investigations (chaired by Representative Peter Kostmayer of Pennsylvania), John Epling, executive director of the New Jersey State Planning Commission, said:

> The public ... wants a balance in its quality of life. It wants well-paying jobs, affordable new homes, and convenient shopping areas as well as accessible open spaces and recreational areas, safe and dynamic cities, clean and potable water, and free-flowing highways. As public officials, however, we often tend to pursue each of these important and worthwhile features in disjointed, uncoordinated ways. We need, at every level of government, a coordinated and integrated set of strategies that manages growth in ways that lead to ... the achievement of many valued goals, not to maximize the achievement of any one goal at the sake of all the others.[23]

Comprehensive state land use planning and regulation again became major issues in several states during the mid-1980s (Delaware, Florida, Maine, New Jersey, Rhode Island, Vermont, and, most recently, Georgia), following a preliminary round of state land use policymaking a decade earlier. These approaches to land use policy have indeed resulted from a variety of problems and policy goals including transportation and other infrastructure needs, the lack of fiscal capacity to meet these requirements, loss of open space and farmland, water and air quality degradation, housing demands, and general economic development objectives.

History

State land use planning and management were conceived in the 1960s and early 70s. Puerto Rico has such a policy that dates back to the years following World War II. Hawaii inaugurated statewide land use planning and regulation in 1961 with direct review of subdivisions and development permits. California followed with its Coastal Commission (1972), and Oregon and Vermont adopted specific environmental guidelines for local land use planning and regulation in the same era. At the time, this trend in state land use policymaking was referred to as the "quiet revolution" in land use planning because of its break with the political and legal tradition of local hegemony over land use. There was a great deal of interest nationally to extend land use planning throughout the country.

Between 1968 and 1975, a national land use policy act was introduced each year in Congress. The act would have established a federal program of financial support for state land use planning similar to what the Coastal Zone Management Act of 1972 provided for coastal areas. That program incorporated certain planning standards and criteria for eligibility to receive the federal funds. Subsequent to the failure of passage of a national land use planning act, the American Law Institute published a model state land use statute in 1977.

Federal Interest in Land Use

The national land use policy act was part of a series of legislative initiatives in Congress that had significant land use implications for the states. Statutes such as the Coastal Zone Management Act, the Clean Water Act, the Clean Air Act, Surface Mine Control and

Reclamation Act, and, most important, the Flood Disaster Protection Act elevated the issue of land use management to a level of political consciousness. By the mid-1970s, however, the political momentum for centralized land use policy had, temporarily at least, exhausted itself. Environmental politics shifted to other issues. On the federal level, land use issues were focused on public lands management, especially as coal mining and oil shale development expanded in the West. Consequently, wilderness designation and National Forest management became priorities.

After President Ronald Reagan's election, environmental advocates went on the defensive for a few years to save environmental achievements from the budget ax and a more conservative political agenda. While environmental innovation by the federal government receded during the Reagan era, the states embarked on a period of environmental activism. Solid and hazardous waste disposal, farmland preservation, wetlands conservation, industrial facility siting, sensitive areas protection, park and recreation land management, and groundwater quality regulation have been the focus of a broad range of state policies. According to Popper, "There is probably more centralized regulation now than there has ever been, but it is also less likely to be comprehensive, more likely to be specialized, oriented to particular purposes." Whether the "combination of even a few single-purpose laws can easily be as effective as a comprehensive land-use law of [the] Florida-Oregon-Vermont sort," as Popper states, is still open to debate.

Resurgence of State Land Use Management

Several of the states that have adopted strict policies in these generic subject areas have also begun to combine single-purpose laws and to integrate their disparate land use-related policies into somewhat integrated comprehensive strategies. New Jersey, for example, has a unique critical areas program (mentioned in chapter five), and hazardous waste, wetlands, coastal zone, and farmland protection policies that other states have used as models. In 1985, New Jersey adopted a bipartisan, statewide land use planning statute. The state planning commission is implementing it and reviewing local land use plans for consistency with those of the state.

Many of the earlier comprehensive statewide land policies have consolidated their political support within recent years. Vermont, for example, revised and strengthened its 1970 Act 250 with Act 200 in 1988. It is ironic, however, that even some municipalities and counties have lobbied state legislatures for more land use regulation. Traditionally, local governments have been the most hostile parties to state usurpation of land use authority.

Political Climate

The reasons for this new political acceptance of land use regulation are many and varied. Even conservative, prodevelopment voters oppose the siting of landfills and power plants in their backyards. The discovery of abandoned hazardous wastes and contaminated groundwater in suburban neighborhoods has created a new environmental consensus. Political supporters of recent statewide land use policies in Florida, New Jersey, and Georgia were odd coalitions of fiscal conservatives, tax revolters, environmentalists, developers, and families seeking the quality of life described by Epling at the beginning of this chapter. In other words, environmental protection is not the *only,* nor the *most* important, rationale for these recent comprehensive statutes.

Florida, for example, found that local governments could not meet the infrastructure needs of a rapidly growing population. Local fiscal capacity was unable to keep up with growing areas which were not paying their own way. At the same time, water sources increasingly were being contaminated by saltwater intrusion and chemical pollutants. Florida's growth management act received extensive support from developers because it was in their interest to find a way for government services to be provided in a timely fashion.

New Jersey was experiencing increasing traffic congestion as suburban and rural areas were developed. Needed highway improvements were so far behind demand that the state began losing business development to Pennsylvania and other states.

Georgia experienced a drought in 1986 during which severe water shortages occurred, brought on in large part by rapid and extensive population growth in the Atlanta metropolitan area during the 1970s and 1980s. The state also found its land use decisions dominated by the courts due to incompatible local land use policies.

Policymakers have identified a wide variety of justifications for statewide comprehensive land use policies. They include improved management of:

- Economic development;
- Wetlands;
- Transportation systems;

- Air quality;
- Water quality;
- Farmland and forests;
- Parks and recreation resources;
- Floodplains;
- Housing demand;
- Wildlife habitat;
- Industrial sites;
- Waste disposal facilities;
- Urban design;
- Fiscal capacity;
- Natural resources and other special areas.

In New Jersey alone, rationale for the state land planning act was variously described to include housing costs, transportation problems, groundwater contamination, air pollution, farmland loss, and a projected deficit of $20 billion in infrastructure financing by the year 2010. Epling described the state's planning act as an authority to address these diverse issues through a "coordinated, integrated and comprehensive growth management strategy."

Economic Development Context

One cause of the dormancy of state land use policy between the mid-1970s and the mid-1980s was the image of its advocates as proponents of growth "control" or, rather, no growth. Many supporters in fact have distanced themselves from any appearance of favoring no growth by reaching out to the prodevelopment community to enlist their support. For example, 1000 Friends of Oregon lobbied aggressively for an amendment to the state's Land Conservation and Development Act to include economic development as an explicit goal for local land use plans. The strategy succeeded by winning the support of the business community and, therefore, mollifying the opponents of state land use law to a significant degree.

John DeGrove, a former Florida state official, has said that definitions of *growth management* range from citizen's efforts to halt growth to rational planning to balance "the needs of the environment with those of development."

The theme of balance seems to be the central objective and ideology of growth management backers. In DeGrove's words,

> The economic recession of the mid-70s, featuring a near-collapse of the construction [and agriculture, energy, min-

ing, forest] industry in some areas, changed the political context within which growth management actors—friend and foe alike—played the game.... The political sophistication of the ... players ... quickly adapted to a position supporting jobs and economic development while at the same time protecting the environment. The catchword became balance, balancing the equally legitimate needs of economic development and environmental protection.[24]

Examples of Growth Management Policies

Whereas every state is unique and the political contexts of states' growth management policies are quite different, some basic similarities exist among various statewide policies.* The new laws generally attempt to integrate an overall state plan that guides state agency plans and local comprehensive plans and regulations. Framing the whole system is the state plan within which all other plans must be consistent.

New Jersey

The state's Land Use Planning Act (P.L. 1985 Chapter 398, {1985}) was stimulated by a ruling issued by the state supreme court involving the township of Mount Laurel.[25] The court's ruling required all local governments to provide for low-income housing through their comprehensive planning authorities. This ruling came in response to a suit filed against the township whose zoning regulations had effectively zoned out low-income housing. The zoning statute had been part of an early growth control ordinance. The court determined to retain direct jurisdiction over all local planning and zoning regulations until the legislature adopted a statewide planning law that addressed New Jersey's housing needs fairly.

Perhaps the more politically decisive issue was traffic congestion and deteriorating transportation infrastructure. State planners estimated a need for $13.8 billion over the next 20 years to accommodate infrastructure needs, only half of which is expected to be available based on current revenue projections.

* Hawaii, Oregon, Delaware, Florida, New Jersey, Maine, Vermont, Georgia, and Rhode Island. A few other states (such as California, New York, Maryland, Virginia, and South Carolina) have regionally administered, special areas land use policies.

Signs of a slowdown in the state's phenomenal growth became apparent when some prominent companies chose other states over New Jersey precisely because the state's infrastructure needs were not being met and growth itself was harming the quality of life. Polls showed popular support for growth management. The combination of these factors created a favorable political climate for passage of the Land Use Planning Act.

The act created the State Planning Commission, which was charged with preparing the State Development and Redevelopment Plan. As in most other growth management acts, New Jersey's requires local governments to prepare plans that are consistent with the state's within a certain period of time, by 1988 in this statute. Of note is language in the act that provides for negotiations among local governing authorities and the state planning office to achieve "cross-compliance" (acceptance) of different plans and consistency with the state plan.

The state legislature wrote explicit, yet broad directions for the plan, which shall:

> a. Protect the natural resources and qualities of the state, including, but not limited to, agricultural development areas, fresh and saltwater wetlands, flood plains, stream corridors, aquifer recharge areas, steep slopes, areas of unique flora and fauna, and areas with scenic, historic, cultural and recreational values;
>
> b. Promote development and redevelopment in a manner consistent with sound planning and where infrastructure can be provided at private expense or with reasonable expenditures of public funds. This should not be construed to give preferential treatment to new construction;
>
> c. Consider input from state, counties and municipal entities concerning their land use, environmental, capital and economic development plans, including to the extent practicable any state plans concerning natural resources or infrastructure elements;
>
> d. Identify areas for growth, limited growth, agriculture, open space conservation and other appropriate designations that the commission may deem necessary;
>
> e. Incorporate a reference guide of technical planning standards and guidelines used in the preparation of the plan; and

f. Coordinate planning activities and establish statewide planning objectives in the following areas: land use, housing, economic development, transportation, natural resource conservation, agriculture and farmland retention, recreation, urban and suburban redevelopment, historic preservation, public facilities and services, and intergovernmental coordination.

Georgia

The Georgia General Assembly passed the most recent land use planning act in March 1989. The growth management bill (HB 215 of 1989 session laws) requires all cities and counties to adopt comprehensive land use plans and zoning laws to implement them. The act enables the state to withhold infrastructure funds from jurisdictions that fail to comply.

The statute also requires local governments to join a regional planning organization. The law created the Governor's Development Council and reorganized the Department of Local (Community) Affairs to monitor compliance. A one-cent sales tax will pay for some of the planning. These funds will be channeled through the regional planning organizations, which will also review and approve local comprehensive plans.

The act closely follows recommendations of the Governor's Growth Strategies Commission, which was created in response to the rapid growth of suburbs around Atlanta and jurisdictional conflicts over water quality relative to wetlands, watersheds, and groundwater recharge areas. The new law also requires local governments to adopt standards to protect these natural resources.

Florida

In 1985, the state legislature consolidated several land use policies under the Growth Management Act and the State Comprehensive Plan. Under the act (Laws of Florida, 85-55), the Governor's Office of Planning and Budgeting reviews state agency and regional plans for consistency with the State Comprehensive Plan. The State Department of Community Affairs reviews local plans and land developments that have a greater than local significance (similar in language to an element of the 1977 American Law Institute's model code). Regional planning councils, strengthened as an intermediate level between local and state governments, can apply substantial sanctions to local governments for failing to develop and submit plans to them and the Department of Community Affairs.

Substantive requirements for local, regional, and state plans include:

(1) Minimizing development on barrier islands and coastal high-hazard areas;
(2) Promoting more compact urban development;
(3) Prohibiting any development for which infrastructure is not already in place.

Plan review and approval are scheduled to occur over a three-year period ending in 1991. Many local plans already have been submitted for review, and some are now in the appellate stage before administrative law judges. The legislature has appointed the Select Committee on Growth Management to oversee this process.

Summary

Polls consistently show that public attitudes strongly favor more, not less, government management of land use activities for environmental objectives. Even constituencies that can be affected economically by state land use regulations favor such actions.

The debate over state land use policy does not appear to be one of growth verses no growth as it was a decade ago. Rather, it seems to be about the kind of development that government *can* support and the kind of environmental quality the public is demanding. Testimony before Congressman Kostmayer's subcommittee consistently pointed to the states as the appropriate level for initiating comprehensive land use planning programs. It appears from the recent enactment of state growth management laws and from the current political climate that more states will be going in this direction. Already Washington, Maryland, Massachusetts, and Virginia have growth strategies commissions studying statewide land use planning proposals. Information sharing among legislatures will be important as state land use policies are formulated and integrated with economic development and fiscal policies.

Although statewide growth policies are finding renewed support, they are not without their critics, some of whom are free market advocates (see chapter seven). But some liberal academics and social policy specialists are raising concerns that need to be weighed in developing state land use planning and conservation programs. For state growth management to succeed, concerns such as affordable housing and local autonomy must be carefully debated.[26]

More than a decade ago, Robert Healy wrote a review of state growth management policies for Resources for the Future. In his preface, he said that the process of policymaking was often one of higher levels of government imposing their will on lower levels of government and that this process tended "to magnify any conceptual mistakes that the original policy might have contained ... [and] has led ... to the spread of policies breathtaking in their insensitivity to local problems and conditions." He continued to say, however, that "the recent movement toward greater state involvement in land use decisions is an exception ... [because] it has ... been initiated in the states themselves, in response to local and statewide needs." This statement can be said about the growth strategies policies of the 1980s as well.

Healy also pointed out in his 1976 report that there was too little experience with state growth management and planning to evaluate their effectiveness. There is now a longer record of experience, but nevertheless a shortage of *objective* policy analyses of growth management programs remains. With the growing interest in these initiatives, it is hoped that better evaluation and analyses will be forthcoming.

VII

Market-Driven Conservation

Since Garrett Hardin published his paper, "Tragedy of the Commons," environmentalists and free market advocates have debated (and sometimes agreed upon) the efficacy of government regulation versus private markets as a means to achieve conservation.[27] Although they do not exactly paraphrase each other, some of those that propose essentially free market conservation policies are Richard Stroup at Montana State, James Hite at Clemson, Gordon Bjork at Claremont Men's College, and William Fischel at Dartmouth. Their general viewpoint is that government bureaucracies are not the most effective or efficient institutions for managing either public or private land for conservation. Some in the environmental community have subscribed to this viewpoint, e.g., U.S. Forest Service plans for timber harvesting have been challenged on the grounds that they are not only wasteful of the resource but also economically unjustified.

Government regulation of land use, according to free marketers, results in economic inefficiencies, political corruption, land speculation, and environmental degradation. Fundamentally, critics of government regulation feel that bureaucracies are more apt to cater to the welfare of their agencies, political sponsors, or allies rather than that of the public. These critics don't oppose all government actions for conservation. They tend to favor corrections in tax policies, creation of artificial markets for environmental values, and minimal regulation at the lowest level of government.

For example, Bjork in *Life, Liberty, and Property* writes:

> Some modification of our institutions controlling land use is needed. The decisions made by individuals (and corporations) about land use do not always result in allocative efficiency. The transactions costs and uncertainties inherent in our present organization of land use are too great. Property rights and zoning practices need to be redefined and re-allocated to conserve and use our natural resources more efficiently.
>
> More action is needed at the local and state level to ensure access by the population to areas of scenic beauty and historic interest. The provision of these public goods should be recognized as a public decision with real costs, and *those costs should be borne by the public and not avoided by uncompensated arbitrary restrictions on the use of property by present owners* [emphasis added].[28]

Some of the arguments by both free marketers and proponents of government regulations are articulated in academic rhetoric and, therefore, are obscure to the lay person. To paraphrase the free market advocates, conservation of special land resources ought to be achieved by paying the landowner for his/her loss of property rights rather than abridging them with regulations. These are essentially the traditional arguments for the respect of pure private property rights.

On the other hand, the free marketers do not adhere to all the principles of Adam Smith. Some recommended changes in free market mechanisms in behalf of conservation are fundamental if not radical changes in the way private land markets have been managed in the past and would require significant government actions to accomplish. In Hite's words:

> Land use in the United States is dictated by the workings of our major social institutions—legal institutions of property rights, institutions of the marketplace, institutions of taxation and public budgetary processes. All of these institutions have deep roots in the American historical experience; all are intertwined and overgrown with the hardy vine of tradition. To an important degree, all of these institutions are finally sanctioned and nourished by government. In any advanced society, land use patterns are an inevitable result of governmental policies toward these basic social institutions. If those patterns are economically wasteful and environmentally unwise, the remedy lies in institutional reform on a broad scale.

> Conventional land-use planning and zoning are merely symptomatic prescriptions that fail to correct the underlying institutional flaws responsible for the problem. If we seriously desire an effective land use policy in the United States, we must be prepared vigorously to cut away some of the vine of tradition in order to repair the basic institutional structure of our society.[29]

Hite suggests some specific policies that are feasible politically and address needs for fundamental changes but in incremental ways. They include:

- Tax credits for conservation management;
- Impact taxes on land development;
- Rational land use planning that incorporates conservation as an explicit capital objective, transfers of development rights, and planned unit developments (PUDs); and
- Improved land use information and access to it.

In fact, use of these policy tools has proceeded faster than Hite imagined it would at the time of his book's publication in 1979.[30] As chapter four describes, tax incentives for wildlife management on private land are used by several states in conjunction with hunting access. Communities in at least 39 states charge impact fees, and some of those states require explicit planning practices by local governments in exchange for the authority to impose those fees. Several states require agencies to administer policies consistent with preserving agricultural land, wetlands, floodplains, and special or sensitive natural areas.

Bjork's recommendations differ from Hite's:

- User fees on public resources (including air and water);
- Replacement of zoning policy with capital planning and government acquisition of parkland;
- Reform of property and income taxes; and
- Marginal pricing for public utilities.

Stroup's market mechanisms for conserving land are similar to Hite's and more familiar to policymakers. They emphasize use of TDRs, purchases of development rights (by government), and conservation easements.

The conventional land market is not without its proponents and successes. The private sector conservation groups, such as the Nature Conservancy, the Trust for Public Lands, and many local land trusts nationwide are significantly increasing the nation's conservation reserves through both fee simple title acquisition as well as conservation easements (see chapter four for a discussion of state policies governing conservation easements).

Land trusts and conservancies are nonprofit organizations dedicated to preservation and management of properties in essentially their natural state. These nonprofits receive donations of land, conservation easements, or money for the purchase of the aforementioned. In return, donors benefit from tax breaks and by knowing that the property will remain undeveloped. Some of these organizations act as intermediaries and turn the properties over to public land conservation agencies. Each transaction is unique, and specific mechanisms for conservation vary according to the needs and legal arrangements on each parcel.

There are other private sector or free market approaches to conservation. For example, the Wildlife Habitat Enhancement Council is an industry-funded organization that manages private properties, mostly corporate ownerships, for wildlife conservation and natural areas preservation. Many corporations such as International Paper and the Anderson-Tully Company manage their forestland holdings not only for timber revenues but also for revenues derived from hunting access. In several cases, profits from recreation access have been documented to exceed, acre for acre, those from other operations such as timber harvesting. Similarly, many farms and ranches are run chiefly for their conservation values.

Hite summarized the rationale for market-driven and private sector land conservation in *Room and Situation:*

> The strengths of market mechanisms are considerable. While there is little real hope that a genuinely free market can be a possibility in twentieth-century America, there are significant opportunities for market mechanisms to be used productively in improving land-use patterns in the United States. The social performance of the land market partakes of the nature of a public good. As such, it is as much a product of political processes as are direct regulations and controls. Market mechanisms have the virtue of dependence not upon centralized, bureaucratic decision making, but decentralized, individual decision making. Reliance upon such mechanisms is both less costly and less destructive of traditional democratic values than direct regulation. For those reasons, the special propensities of Adam Smith's invisible hand deserve to be kept firmly in mind as land-use policy alternatives are debated in the political arena.[31]

Market mechanisms, such as user's fees, are being increasingly experimented with to achieve environmental quality objectives. They seem to hold most promise when they augment public regulatory policy and are directed at managing resources. Whether they are as effective at land conservation as their proponents maintain is unclear. Market mechanisms such as transfers of development rights and wetlands banking are complex to administer and may have to overcome other influences on land use such as taxes, zoning, and capital development planning.

VIII

Conclusion

This book has been written primarily for the legislative audience and, therefore, has emphasized the governmental role in land conservation. Debates about government action are characterized by arguments over regulation of private property rights. In the heat of these debates, we forget the significant role that government plays as an enabler. Land use and conservation are no exception. The most exciting programs in land conservation today are the special areas or management projects where government and the private sector cooperate. Sometimes this scenario may occur with a degree of government coercion; sometimes cooperation results from private sector representatives inviting government to assist in achieving one objective or another.

Hite says that "to consider managing the environment without a well-thought-out, effective land-use policy is to indulge oneself in the wildest of fantasies." This statement begs the question: whose land use policy? Hite's statement implies that we have no land use policy. But we do. It is a highly complex set of policies. In essence, our system of land policies has evolved and is structured to manage the multitude of conflicts that arise when we cannot agree over how best to manage specific areas.

Zoning, the basic American system for land use decision making, is intended to separate conflicting uses and rationally organize human economic and social activities to minimize incompatible land uses, thus reducing social conflicts. Because variances are relatively easy to obtain and land use plans frequently are arbitrary, zoning has been criticized by liberals and conservatives alike. But the criticism of zoning, and hence government regulation of land use, illustrates the inconsistencies in political beliefs. Although liberals traditionally oppose centralized power, they also advocate a more rational, planned use of the land. Conservatives' support for undiminished individual property rights may stymie the economic development they favor.

Efforts to establish comprehensive land use planning policies in the 1970s raised a torrent of opposition. Ironically, recent legislation for comprehensive land use policies has gained surprising consensus. Likewise, support for conservation of land resources is strong. We are moving toward a more conservative, albeit conservationist, attitude about land use. Will we be more circumspect, however, in adopting new land policies than we have in the past? If we fine tune zoning but ignore property taxes, if we expand our use of conservation easements but do nothing regarding environmental performance standards, will we truly improve land conservation practices?

Any single land use policy generally has a number of proponents with multiple objectives that frequently conflict. Likewise, there are internal contradictions over the efficacy of any particular conservation action. For example, the National Park Service is trying to save a population of mountain goats (a rare animal) in the Olympic National Park. Ironically, the goats are apparently destroying some rare plants. Conservationists are faced with the dilemma of choosing which rare species will be favored by management. Similar dilemmas have occurred over wild horses and burros depleting native plants and game populations. Reclaiming mined lands by growing native plants that do not germinate easily or by introducing less desirable plants that survive and hold the soil has been an issue of contention. In another debate, those who support recycling plastics have squared off against those who promote development and manufacturing of biodegradable plastics.

Land use decision making breeds conflict. A number of institutions and organizations specialize in mediating or managing conflicts such as those that arise over land use and related conservation issues. The Harvard Program on Negotiation, George Mason University's Conflict Clinic, the Keystone Center in Colorado, and the Mediation Institute in Seattle are just a few. But no model for state land conservation policy exists that provides an ideal solution for conflicts or conservation dilemmas. The examples presented in the preceding chapters afford a variety of incremental steps toward conservation of important land resources. Many experts recommend that states consider integrating land use goals by developing more comprehensive policies, such as growth strategies acts. Other experts, political economists on both the left and the right, argue that land use and conservation are inextricably tied to American tax law and the structure of our economy. Without addressing these fundamental areas, they reason, land use planning laws and regulations will not succeed and may even cause further resource degradation.

There is a place for both government regulation and free market processes to achieve conservation objectives. In fact, most states use a mixture of market and regulatory approaches. A great deal of experimentation is going on nationwide, and although the ensuing conflicts may be painful and difficult for politicians and the interests involved in these conflicts, they are inevitable and necessary. Perhaps effective means to conserve valuable resources are not possible without conflict. To search for comprehensive panaceas to resolve conservation issues permanently is probably futile.

Ideological purity and academic status should not be the primary criteria for action. Practicality, effectiveness, and cost should be the criteria for developing conservation programs. Tradeoffs are inevitable. Some property rights will be diminished; some critical areas and endangered species will be lost. The test of conservation policy is not whether it is perfect but whether it is reasonable.

Appendix
Information Resources

Carol Baudler
The Nature Conservancy
Government Relations
1800 North Kent Street
Arlington, VA 22209
(703) 841-5358

David Brower
Center for Urban and Regional Studies
University of North Carolina
108 Battle Lane
Chapel Hill, NC 27514
(919) 962-3074

Benjamin Chinitz
Lincoln Institute of Land Policy
26 Trowbridge Street
Cambridge, MA 02138
(617) 661-3016

John DeGrove
Joint Center for Environmental and Urban Problems
Florida Atlantic University/Florida International University
500 N.W. 20th Street
Boca Raton, FL 33431
(305) 355-5270

J. Glenn Eugster
Division of Park and Resource Planning
National Park Service
600 Arch St., Room 9428
Philadelphia, PA 19106
(215) 597-7386

Bob Gray
Resource Management Consultants, Inc.
1920 N Street, N.W.
Suite 400A
Washington, DC 20036
(202) 857-0209

Jean Hocker
Land Trust Exchange
1017 Duke Street
Alexandria, VA 22314
(703) 683-7778

Harvey Jacobs
Department of Urban and Regional Planning
University of Wisconsin
925 Bascom Hall, Music Hall
Madison, WI 53706
(608) 262-1004

Larry Jahn
Wildlife Management Institute
Suite 725
1101 14th St., N.W.
Washington, DC 20005
(202) 371-1808

Jon Kustler
Association of Wetland Managers
Box 2463
Berne, NY 12023
(518) 872-1804

Phyllis Myers
State Resource Strategies
3248 Patterson St., N.W.
Washington, DC 20015
(202) 362-5212

Frank Popper
Department of Urban Studies and Community H
Rutgers University of New Jersey
Lucy Stone Hall
New Brunswick, NJ 08903
(201) 932-4009

Luther Propst
Successful Communities Program
The Conservation Foundation
1250 Twenty-fourth St., N.W.
Washington, DC 20037
(202) 778-9637

Henry Richmond
1000 Friends of Oregon
300 Willamette Building
534 Southwest Third Avenue
Portland, OR 97204
(503) 223-4396

Notes

1. Hugh Ulrich, *Losing Ground: Agricultural Policy and the Decline of the American Farm* (Chicago, Ill.: Chicago Review Press, 1989), p. 57.
2. Sidney Plotkin, *Keep Out: The Struggle for Land Use Control* (Berkeley, Calif.: University of California Press, 1987), p. 11.
3. A. S. Mather, *Land Use* (New York, N.Y.: Longman Group U.K. Limited, 1986), p. 62.
4. Frank J. Popper, "Understanding American Land-Use Regulation Since 1970: A Revisionist Interpretation," *Journal of the American Planning Association* 54, no. 3 (Summer 1988): 299.
5. Peter Wolf, *Land in America: Its Value, Use and Control* (New York, N.Y.: Pantheon, 1981), p. 51.
6. Ibid., p. 64.
7. James C. Hite, *Room and Situation: The Political Economy of Land-Use Policy* (Chicago: Nelson-Hall, 1979), pp. 75-76.
8. Wolf, *Land in America,* p. 81.
9. John Stuart Mill, *Principles of Political Economy* (New York, N.Y.: Augustus M. Kelley, 1965), reprint, pp. 444-448.
10. Wolf, *Land in America,* p. 86.
11. *Berman v. Parker,* 348 U.S. 26, 75 S. Ct. 98, 99 L. Ed. 27 (1954).
12. *Moviematic Industries Corp. v. Bd. of County Commissioners of Metropolitan Dade County,* 349 So. 2d 667 (Fla. 3d D.C.A. 1977).
13. *Graham v. Estuary Properties,* 399 So. 2d 1372 (Fla. 1981), *cert. denied,* 454 U.S. 1083 (1981).
14. *Just v. Marinette County,* 201 N.W. 2d 761 (Wis. 1972).
15. *Euclid v. Ambler Realty Co.,* 272 U.S. 365, 388 (1926).
16. *Pennsylvania Coal Co. v. Mahon,* 260 U.S. 393 (1922).
17. Sherry Lynn Jacobs, "Strengthening Wetland Protection Programs Through State Regulation," *University of California Davis Law Review* 21, p. 227.
18. *Farmland Notes* (Washington, D.C.: National Association of State Departments of Agriculture Farmland Project, January 1987).
19. Janet Diehl and Thomas Barrett, *The Conservation Easement Handbook: Managing Land Conservation and Historic Preservation Easement Programs* (Alexandria, Va.: Land Trust Exchange and Trust for Public Land, 1988).
20. National Conference of Commissioners on Uniform State Laws, *1988-89 Reference Book* (Chicago, Ill.: National Conference of Commissioners on Uniform State Laws, 1989), p. 102.
21. Rich Clough, Barbara Sheline, and Barb Lloyd, "Compensation to Landowners for Recreational Access—A Survey of All State Programs" (Helena, Mont.: Montana Department of Fish, Wildlife, and Parks, 1986).
22. Popper, "Understanding American Land Use Regulation," p. 296.
23. John W. Epling, Testimony to the Subcommittee on General Oversight and Investigations, Committee on Interior and Insular Affairs, United States House of Representatives, May 18, 1989.
24. John M. DeGrove, "Growth Management and Governance," paper prepared for Research Gaps in Growth Management Conference, Alexandria, Virginia, September 9-10, 1988.
25. *Southern Burlington County NAACP v. Township of Mount Laurel,* 456 A. 2nd 713 (1983).

26. For further information on these issues, see Christine Minnehan, "When Worlds Collide: Managing Growth and Meeting Housing Needs," in *Domestic Agenda for the 90s: State Leaders Define the Choices,* Report of the Intergovernmental Affairs Committee (Lexington, Ky.: Council of State Governments, 1989), pp. 51-58; and Harvey M. Jacobs, "Localism and Land Use Planning," *The Journal of Architectural and Planning Research* 6, no. 1 (Spring 1989).

27. Garrett Hardin, "The Tragedy of the Commons," *Science* 162 (1968): 1243-1248.

28. Gordon C. Bjork, *Life, Liberty, and Property: The Economics and Politics of Land-Use Planning and Environmental Controls* (Lexington, Mass.: D.C. Heath & Co., 1980), pp. 18-19.

29. Hite, *Room and Situation,* pp. viii-ix.

30. James Hite, December 12, 1989: personal interview.

31. Hite, *Room and Situation,* pp. 132-133.

References

American Law Institute. *A Model Land Development Code.* Philadelphia, Pa.: American Law Institute, 1977.

Andrews, Richard N. L., ed. *Land in America: Commodity or Resource?* Lexington, Mass.: D.C. Heath & Co., 1979.

Baudler, Carol Lee, and Loop, Donna. "State Funding for Natural Areas: Progress Report." Memorandum. Arlington, Va.: The Nature Conservancy, November 1989.

Benson, Ann. "Catching Up on Growth Management." *Urban Land,* January 1988.

Bjork, Gordon C. *Life, Liberty, and Property: The Economics and Politics of Land Use Planning and Environmental Controls.* Lexington, Mass.: D.C. Heath & Co., 1980.

Brenneman, Russell L., and Bates, Sarah M. *Land-Saving Action: A Written Symposium by 29 Experts on Private Land Conservation in the 1980s.* Covelo, Calif.: Island Press, 1984.

Church, W. L. "Private Lands and Public Recreation: A Report and Proposed New Model Act on Access, Liability and Trespass." Washington, D.C.: National Association of Conservation Districts et al., 1979.

Clough, Rich; Sheline, Barbara; and Lloyd, Barb. "Compensation to Landowners for Recreational Access—A Survey of All State Programs." Helena, Mont.: Montana Department of Fish, Wildlife, and Parks, 1986.

Conard, Rebecca Ann. "The Conservation of Local Autonomy: California's Agricultural Land Policies, 1900-1966." Ph.D. dissertation. Santa Barbara, Calif.: University of California, 1984. [Especially chapter six, "American Federalism: The State-Local Dimension," pp. 249-278.]

Corbett, Marjorie R., ed. *Greenline Parks: Land Conservation Trends for the Eighties and Beyond.* Washington, D.C.: National Parks and Conservation Association, 1984.

Davidson, Jonathan M. "Plan-Based Land Development and Infrastructure Controls: New Directives for Growth Management." *Journal of Land Use and Environmental Land* 2, no. 2.

DeGrove, John M. "Growth Management and Governance." Paper prepared for Research Gaps in Growth Management Conference, Alexandria, Va., September 9-10, 1988.

__________. *Land, Growth and Politics.* Chicago, Ill.: American Planning Association, 1984.

Diehl, Janet, and Barrett, Thomas. *The Conservation Easement Handbook: Managing Land Conservation and Historic Preservation Easement Programs.* Alexandria, Va.: Land Trust Exchange and Trust for Public Land, 1988.

Dillard, Jan Elizabeth. "Determinants of State Land Use Policies: A Comparative State Policy Study." Ph.D. dissertation. Atlanta, Ga.: Emory University, 1982.

Epling, John W. Testimony to the Subcommittee on General Oversight and Investigations, Committee on Interior and Insular Affairs, United States House of Representatives, May 18, 1989.

Farmland Notes. Washington, D.C.: National Association of State Departments of Agriculture Farmland Project, January 1987.

Folwell, Elizabeth. "Present at the Creation." *Adirondack Life* XX, no. 4 (July/August 1989): 56-119.

Foster, Stephen K. "The Determinants of Innovation in State Growth Management Policy." Ph.D. dissertation. Tallahassee, Fla.: Florida State University, 1983.

Fulton, William. "In Land-Use Planning, a Second Revolution Shifts Control to the States." *Governing* (March 1989): 40-45.

Guskind, Robert. "New Jersey Says 'Enough': A New State Plan Is Being Hailed as a Political Turnabout." *Planning* (June 1988): 24-30.

Hamann, Richard. "Wetland Regulation." In *4 Rohan, Zoning and Land Use Controls.* New York, N.Y.: Matthew Bender & Co., Inc., 1988.

Healy, Robert G. *Land Use and the States.* Baltimore, Md.: Johns Hopkins University Press, 1976.

Hiemstra, Hal, and Bushwick, Nancy, eds. *Plowing the Urban Fringe.* Boca Raton, Fla.: Florida Atlantic University/Florida International University Joint Center for Environmental and Urban Problems, 1988.

Hite, James C. *Room and Situation: The Political Economy of Land-Use Policy.* Chicago, Ill.: Nelson-Hall, 1979.

Jacobs, Sherry Lynn. "Strengthening Wetland Protection Programs Through State Regulation." *University of California Davis Law Review* 21, p. 227.

Kusler, Jon A. *Regulating Sensitive Lands: A Guidebook.* Cambridge, Mass.: Ballinger Publishing Company, 1980.

Kusler, Jon A., and Hamann, Richard, eds. *Wetland Protection: Strengthening the Role of the States.* Proceedings of a national symposium for the Association of State Wetland Managers and Center for Government Responsibility. University of Florida College of Law, Gainesville, Fla., September 19-21, 1984.

Laitin, Jon. "Down East Drama: Will a New State Law Help the Little Guys Stand Up to the Big Time Developers? Stay Tuned." *Planning* (August 1988): 21-24.

Land Letter. Washington, D.C.: W. J. Chandler Associates newsletter.

Mandelker, Daniel R. *Environment and Equity: A Regulatory Challenge.* New York, N.Y.: McGraw-Hill, 1981.

Mather, A. S. *Land Use.* New York, N.Y.: Longman Group U.K. Limited, 1986.

Meeks, Gordon Jr. *Managing Environmental and Public Policy Conflicts: A Legislator's Guide.* Denver, Colo.: National Conference of State Legislatures, 1985.

__________. "Multiple Use Management on Private Lands: Private Revenue and Public Benefits." *State Legislative Report.* Denver, Colo.: National Conference of State Legislatures, February 1986.

Meeks, Gordon Jr., and Runyon, Cheryl. *Wetlands Preservation and the States.* Denver, Colo.: National Conference of State Legislatures, 1990.

Merrill, Lorraine Stuart. "The Road Not Taken: Two New England States Have Taken Widely Different Approaches to Planning and Development—With Surprisingly Similar Results." *Planning* (November 1987): 22-24.

Molnar, William E. "A Review of Comprehensive Land Use Policy Structure." Report prepared for the State Planning and Community Affairs Committee, Georgia State House of Representatives, June 6, 1988.

Morandi, Larry. *Environmental Use: A Reappraisal of Balance.* Denver, Colo.: National Conference of State Legislatures, 1985.

__________. *State Groundwater Protection Policies: A Legislator's Guide.* Denver, Colo.: National Conference of State Legislatures, 1989.

Morandi, Larry; Meeks, Gordon; and Sacarto, Douglas. *Land Management: Sustaining Resource Values.* Denver, Colo.: National Conference of State Legislatures, 1983.

Myers, Phyllis, and Green, Sharon N. *State Parks in a New Era.* Washington, D.C.: The Conservation Foundation, 1989.

"Non-Traditional Sources of Revenue & Innovative Utilization of Funds for Parks and Outdoor Recreation: A Survey of the States." Alexandria, Va.: The National Recreation and Park Association, 1986.

Plotkin, Sidney. *Keep Out: The Struggle for Land Use Control.* Berkeley, Calif.: University of California Press, 1987.

Popper, Frank J. "Understanding American Land-Use Regulation Since 1970: A Revisionist Interpretation." *Journal of the American Planning Association* 54, no. 3 (Summer 1988): 291-301.

President's Commission on Americans Outdoors. *American Outdoors: The Legacy, The Challenge.* Washington, D.C.: Island Press, 1987.

Sanders, Steve. "Does California Need a Policy to Manage Urban Growth?" Report from the Senate Urban Growth Policy Project. Sacramento, Calif.: California Senate Office of Research, 1989.

Stephens, Jack L. "Conservation Easements: The Georgia Experience." Atlanta, Ga.: Georgia House of Representatives, 1989.

Stroup, Richard L. "The Political Control of Rural Land in Oregon: A Policy Analysis." Working Paper 89-1. Bozeman, Mont.: Political Economy Research Center, Montana State University, 1989.

Tarlock, Dan A. "State Siting Laws, Local Land Use Laws, and Their Interplay." *Environmental Law Reporter* 15 (August 1985): 10236-10239.

Williams, Norman Jr., and Taylor, John. *American Planning Law: Land Use and the Police Power.* Vol. 5, Sections 157, 158, 159, and 160 et seq. Wilmette, Ill.: Callaghan & Co., 1985 Revision, cumulative.

Wolf, Peter. *Land in America: Its Value, Use and Control.* New York, N.Y.: Pantheon, 1981.